# Table of Contents

**1. City Summary** (3)

**2. Transportation** (5)

**3. Attractions** (9~66)

(1) Pantai Cenang (11)

(2) Oriental Village (16)

(3) Tanjung Rhu Beach (28)

(4) Kuah Town (40)

(5) Eagle Square & Jetty Point (52)

(6) Legend Park & Chogm Park (62)

(Than Jung Rhu Beach)

(Oriental Village)

(Pantai Cenang Beach)

## (1) City Summary

Langkawi is an island located at northern region of Malaysia and is near to Penang Island. The size of Langkawi is near to double of Penang, but the number of people in Langkawi is much smaller than that of Penang. According to a taxi driver, population is only 1/10 of Penang's due to government policy to preserve the nature on Langkawi Island rather than developing it like Penang which has many manufacturing factories. Therefore, the air cleanness and landscape in Langkawi, is superb. Instead of developing the island, government designated Langkawi as a duty-free region as a compensation for no development.

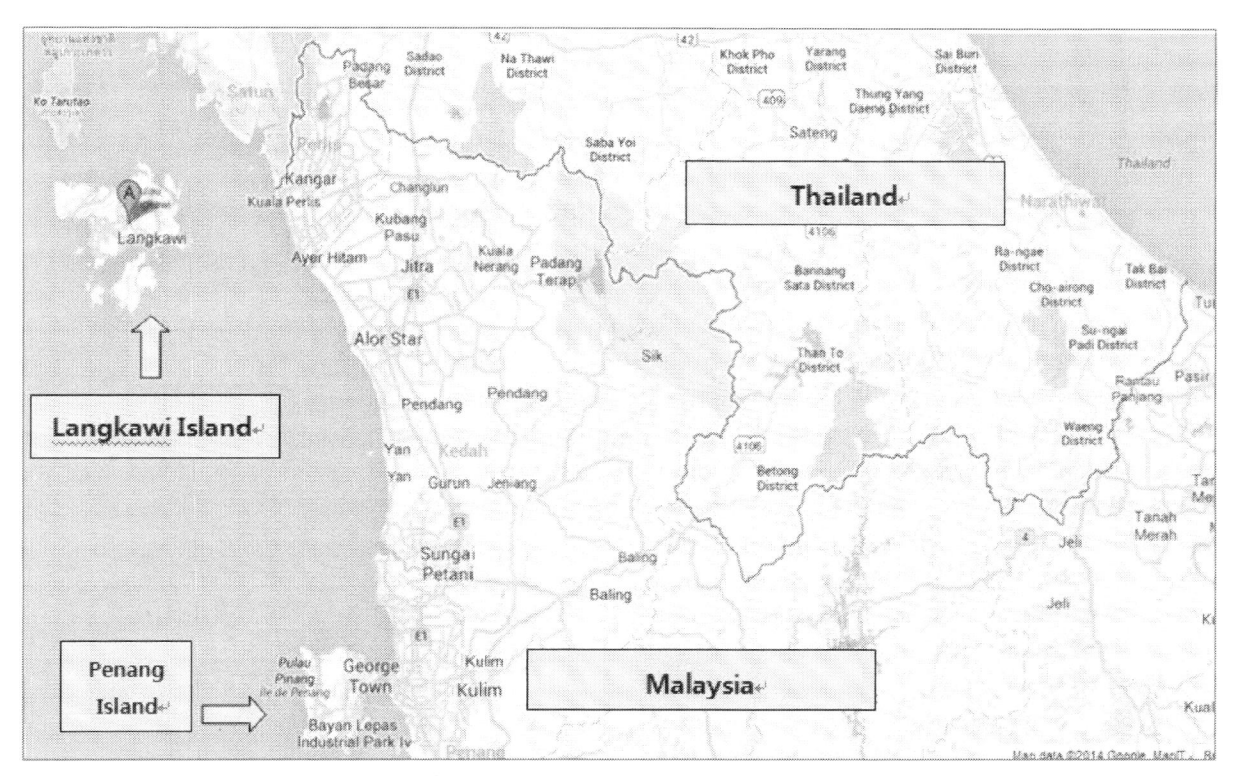

**Duty Free** : You can enjoy duty free at any shop in Lanakawi. However, you will not be able to find other than 3 items. Chocolate, liquor and cigarette. They are all, if I say strongly about items you can buy duty freely. However, you will see various kind of chocolate, numerous liquor and tabacco at shops.

**Downtown** : There are 2 downtowns at Langkawi. Pentai Cenang and Kuah Town. However, Pantai Cenang is more recommendable one. Activities such as swimming, boating and tanning are easy taken at the beaches located just in front of the rear door of the hotels in Pantai Cenang. Airport and attractions such as Oriental Village, 7 Waterfalls and Tanjung Rhu beach, are also located near Pantai Cenang. Shops, restaurants, fast food stores like KFC, Mcdonalds, are easily accessible too. Therefore, reservation for lodges at Pantai Cenang, is more recommendable than at Kuah Town.

Kuah Town has also many local restaurants, mall of Langkawi Parade and attractions such as Eagle Square (Eagle is the symbol of Langkawi), Legend Park and Jetty Point where you can take ferries to Penang Island and Thai islands.

The biggest mall at Kuah Town, is Langkawi Parade. Langkawi Parade is located at the entrance of Kuah Town but a little far from centre of Kuah Town. According to taxi driver, you can not get fruits except season of harvest. Here is the information about Langkawi Parade. 潮順發 in Chinese and you can read "Teow Soon Huat". Address : A14~15, Pokok Asam, Juah 07000 Pulau Langkawi, Malaysia. Tel : 604 – 966-5017/5018.

Map of Langkawi.

## (2) Transportation

Langkawi Airport.

In contrast with Penang, there is no city bus for travelers to be able to take for the access to attractions. There are buses running for local people from residence to residence, I heard. However, according to my experience, you'd better give up catching buses at Langkawi. I can not avoid to say that taxi and rent-a-car are all for travelers. Therefore, you have to take a taxi from airport to your lodge.

**(How to take a taxi at airport & how to rent a car)**

**Taxi** has no taximeter. Taxi fare must be negotiated except at airport. There is a taxi ticket box at airport. It is located at the left hand when you see the exit door at the airport after collecting your luggage. Tell your hotel name to the staff at the taxi box and he/she will give you a ticket for boarding. If you suggest your taxi ticket to another counter located outside door, they will mark down taxi number on the ticket for you to take. In my case, I paid RM30 for the ticket to hotel at Kuah Town. Therefore, RM20 ~ RM30 would be enough for any hotel from the airport. Pentai Cenang is much closer than Kuah Town from airport. Therefore, RM20 would be enough for hotels at Pantai Cenang.

**Rent-a-car** offices at airport are sitting at right side of the concierge when you see the exit door of airport after collecting your luggage. If you want to rent a car, you will negotiate rent fee at any rent-a-car office at airport. And you may also rent a car at your hotel. For your reference, I've negotiated rental fee down to RM80(around US$25) for a small car for 24 hours when they suggested RM120 at first.

Arrival Hall of Langkawi Airport. Many car rental booths are waiting at the right side of corridor. Taxi ticket counter is located on your left. Tell your hotel name to the staff at the taxi counter, he/she will issue a ticket. Then, receive taxi number at another taxi counter behind the exit doors of arrival hall. Considering RM30 to hotel at Kuah Town where is a long distance from airport, RM20 would be enough for the hotels at Pantai Cenang.

Show your taxi ticket to another taxi booth located outside arrival hall of airport. They will endow a taxi number to ride. A taxi driver will approach you to serve to your hotel.

**(Cars & gas stations in Malaysia)**

Cars in Malaysia have driver's seat on the right and run on the left lane of road. Therefore, it is a little confusing for the driver's who is accustomed to left-hand cars and to drive on the left lane on the street. However, you don't need to worry if you are a holder of international driving license. Five minutes for adaption to something strange, will let you feel free from your worry.

Negotiate the rental price at a rent-a-car office located at airport for a small car(around 1,600 cc). If you are asked more than RM80 for 24 hours, do not hesitate to go another rental booth. Your hotel also will arrange for you a rent-a-car at front desk.

Gas price in Malaysia, one of the oil-producing countries, is really cheap. RM30, approximately US$10, for 14 liter of gasoline, will allow you to take a whole look around the island and it will be left in the tank when you return the car. When you receive a rent-a-car, drive to a gas station first. You can easily find a station near the spot you have received car through a map of Langkawi collectable at hotels or airport. Gas stations in Langkawi, are self-service filling stations. Pay first at cashier and fill the tank by yourself. No refund will be made for the remaining fuel when you return the car to the rental company. A bill at gas station showing gas price is shown below. RM30 for 14.29 liter.

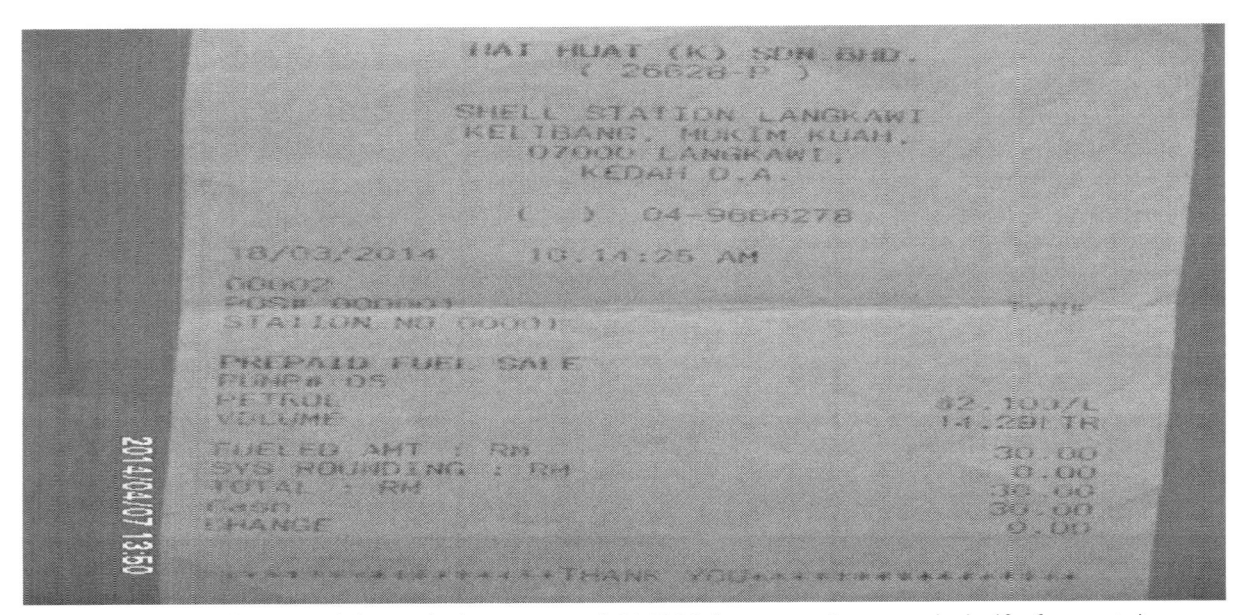

In my case, a staff at hotel front desk suggested RM120 for a small car on behalf of a rental company for 24 hours when I asked him to arrange a rent-a-car. After carefully listening to my explaining of my friend's case who rented a car at RM80 yesterday, he discussed the price with someone on the phone and finally accepted RM80. At 10 a.m. next morning, a staff from a rental company handed over a car to me with his business card. The staff asked me to deposit another RM120 for any damage to the car caused by myself. I also claimed to the staff that RM120 has to be repaid early next morning due to my flight to Johor Bahru. RM120 was paid back to me at 9 a.m. next morning through hotel front desk when I return the key to the front.

A rent car. 5 doors. RM80 for 24 hours. Good air conditioner, nothing to be required more. Perfect.

## (3) Attractions

Attractions at Langkawi Island can be largely divided into 3 places. The first one is Pantai Cenang which is crowded with tourists, hotels, restaurants and malls. Pantai Cenang located close to airport, has beaches for travelers to enjoy outdoor activities on the sea such as swimming and boating. And Oriental Village, one of the best attractions at Langkawi, is situated near Pantai Cenang.

The second is Kuah Town. It's a short trip to Jetty Point where you can take ferries to various islands located near to Langkawi. Eagle Square (Eagle is the symbol of Langkawi) is also near to Kuah Town. You can take a look at Legend Park and Chogm Park just in 5 minutes by car from Eagle Square. Tanjung Rhu Beach area can be recommended as the final one of the attractions at Langkawi. You will meet a calm and beautiful beach to enjoy swimming and getting a tan under the blasting sun.

This book will take a look at (a) Pantai Cenang first which is the nearest place from airport and most bustling town at Langkawi. Then, you will go to (b) Oriental Village to take cable cars up to the top of the mountain behind the village. Seven Wells Waterfall must not be skipped after Oriental Village. After swimming at the silent beach of (c) Tanjung Rhu, we will move to (d) Kuah Town. And, (e) Eagle Square and Jetty Point will be visited before (f) Legend Park and Chogm Park. Now, let's go to find the 6 attractions at Langkawi with photos.

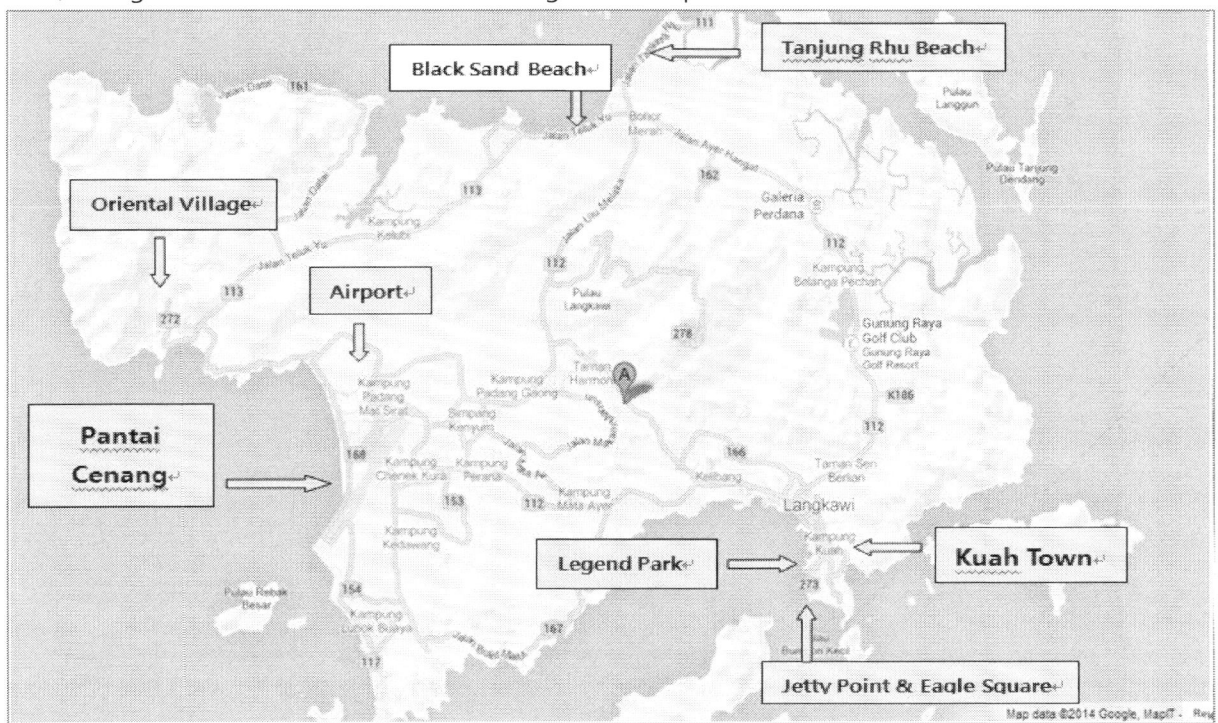

Spot points of Langkawi.

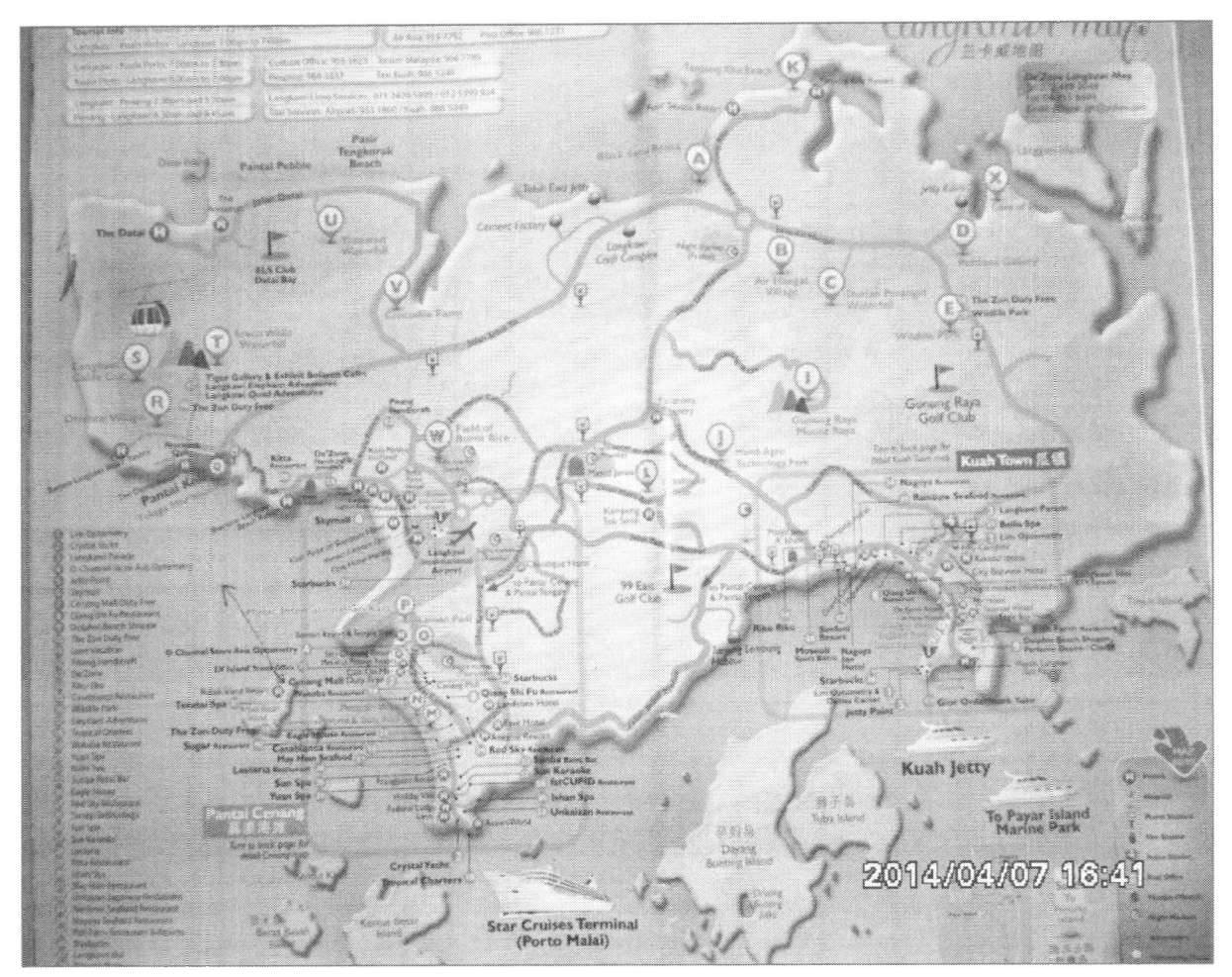

The red rectangular box on the left of the map, shows the area of Pantai Cenang. Another rectangular one on the right, is Kuah Town.

## (1) Pantai Cenang

Pantai Cenang is located near from airport. It's the most bustling town at Langkawi. It does not take long to Oriental Village either which has cable cars to go to the top of the mountain behind the village. Seven Wells Waterfall where you can enjoy trails to the top, is located just 20 minutes on foot from Oriental Village.

If you book a hotel near the beach at Pantai Cenang, there you can enjoy Cenang beach just through the rear doors of the hotel. There are so many restaurants, fast food stores such as KFC and Mcdonalds, many convenient stores and supermarkets. Even though it is difficult for you to move far without taking a taxi or a rent car, considering its location from the attractions and airport, Pantai Cenang is the most recommendable place at this island.

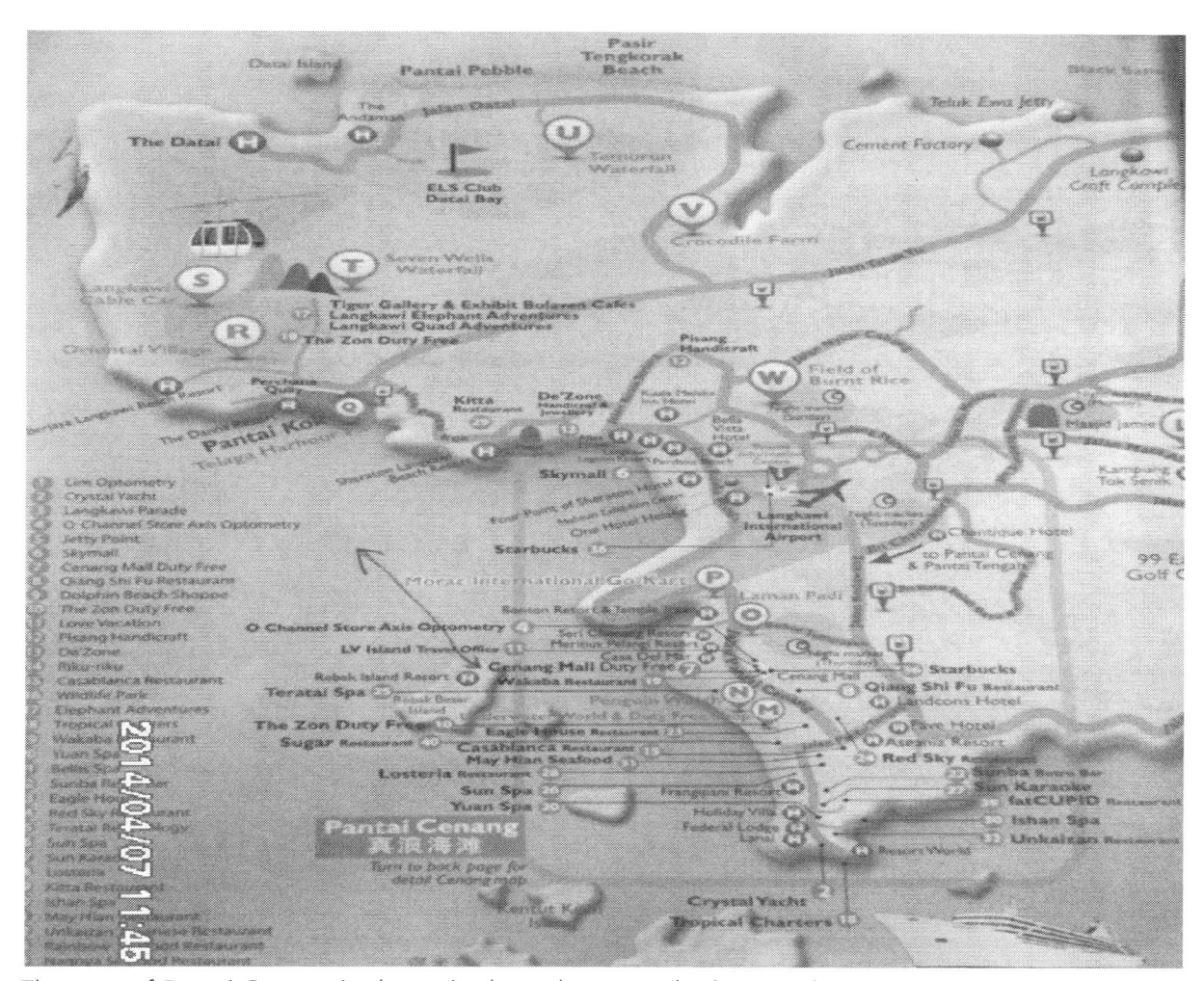

The area of Pantai Cenang is shown in the red rectangular box on the map.

KFC and Mcdonalds in the centre of Pantai Cenang. Motorcycling is little recommended under the hot sun.

Cenang Beach just across the road from KFC. Beach parasols and boats are waiting.

Entry to the Beach.

Beach Parasols and boats are waiting for travelers at Pantai Cenang beach.

Boats floating around the swimming beach surrounded by a shark net.

Speed boats and beach parasols.

Left side of Cenang Beach.

Swimming on the sea and tanning on the sand.

**(2) Oriental Village & Seven Wells Waterfall**

Oriental Village is located near Pantai Cenang. Cable cars between Oriental Village and the top of the mountain surrounding the village, will allow you to enjoy the open scenery from the view points on the top. Oriental Village situated at north-western side of Langkawi, is also near Seven Wells Waterfall where you can experience trails to the top of the mountain.

Regardless of the hotel situation whether at Pantai Cenang or at Kuah Town, you have to take a taxi to go Oriental Village. However, you can reach Seven Wells Waterfall from the village on foot. 20 minutes walking from Oriental Village, would be enough to the waterfall. Taxi fare from Kuah Town to Oriental Village, was RM42. The distance between Kuah Town which is located at south-eastern district of Langkawi and Oriental Village situated at north-western area, is quite long.

RM42 for a taxi fare to Oriental Village, seems not too expensive if you take look at the beautiful settlings in Oriental Village and panoramic views from the top of the mountain. You are recommended to take as many photos as you can before riding a cable car to the top.

There are 2 stops on the way to the top. Do not alight the cable car at the first stop called middle station. Go to the final station directly. After enjoying the scenery from the top first, you'd better stop by the middle station on the way to return to the village. RM30 for a round trip. Now, let's go to Oriental Village and Seven Wells Waterfall with a camera.

Parking lot at the entrance to Oriental Village.

Through the bridge over there. Free entry.

Suspension bridges to the village. Left one to enter and right one for your return. "Selamat Datang" on the signboard means "Welcome".

Oriental Village.

Cute houses.

Cable car station in front. Get a ticket and go upstairs to take a cable car to the top of mountain seen behind.

Ticket window is on the right side of house.

Queue at upstairs to take a cable car.

Boarding gate. A crew who takes photo of us without prior permission, asks to buy it. You will see numbers on the floor from 1 to 8 at boarding line not to exceed the capacity of a cable car.

Middle Station. Do not alight the cable car at this station. Go straight to the next station.

Middle Station  If you've alighted here, you can take another cable car to go to the top.

Observation deck at the final station seen on the top of the mountain.

Observation deck at Middle Station.

Observatory at middle station.

A cable car is flying up to the final station on the top of the mountain.

Small but comfortable.

Cable cars between Middle Station and the final station at the top.

The final station at the top.

On a fine day, if you stand here around 7 p.m., the most wonderful sunset will show you itself.

Observatory platform at the top.

Entry to Seven Wells Waterfall. Around 20 minutes on foot from Oriental Village.

You can experience trails at Seven Wells Waterfall.

A parking lot at Seven Wells Waterfall on the right.

RM2 for cars, RM1 for motorcycles.

## (3) Tanjung Rhu Beach

Tanjung Rhu Beach is located at north-eastern area of Langkawi. When you drive a rent car, follow the main road to the Tanjung Rhu Beach after taking a look at Oriental Village and Seven Wells Waterfall. You will not get lost on the way to the beach if you follow direction signs on the road to Tanjung Rhu.

You can experience various activities at the beach such as swimming, tanning, mangrove experiment, snorkeling and so on. For mangrove experiment and snorkeling, you will meet a signpost standing at a parking lot of the beach.

When you drive for 20 minutes along the main road from Seven Wells Waterfall to the direction of Tanjung Rhu Beach, you will meet 2 other beaches on your left.

A beach on the way to Tanjug Rhu Beach. This sands extend to Black Sand Beach.

A rent car is parking under a tree on the way to Tanjung Rhu Beach.

This is a compact car rented at RM80 and filled with 14 liters of gasoline at RM30.

This beach has a rest area with pavilions on the right. If you have swimming suit, please do not hesitate to dive here right now. When I revisited here at 5 p.m. swimming was impossible due to the withdrawal of the sea far away.

A beach by the road on the way to Tanjung Rhu Beach.

This beach seems to reach to Black Sand Beach on the right.

The long beach is sitting on the left of the road. Drive this road to Tanjung Rhu Beach and you will meet Black Sand Beach on your left in 10 minutes from here.

The beach by the road, stretches its sands endlessly like this. You cannot see the end of the sands with naked eyes. White tents seen far right, may be standing at Black Sand Beach. You have to go further for Tanjung Rhu Beach through the road on the right.

The long beach looked back. Endless white sands.

Parking lot at the entrance to Tanjung Rhu Beach. Monkeys run here and there.

A signboard standing at the parking lot. For boat activities such as mangrove tour, snorkeling and fishing, go to the right. For swimming, go to the left, opposite direction to the signpost.

Entrance to Tanjong Rhu Beach.

Shops and restaurants are sitting by a giant tree standing at the entrance of Tanjong Rhu Beach.

Tanjong Rhu Beach lies behind the signpost on the tree. The counter under the red roof in front, sells boat activities. Local restaurants are on the right.

Signpost says Tanjong Rhu Beach.

Tanjung Rhu Beach.

Tanning on the sands under the blazing sun.

Swimming, tanning and boating.

Entrance looked back from the beach.

A signboard standing on the left of the entrance. "Pool and chairs only for house guests."

Shops at the entrance of the beach.

### (4) Kuah Town

Drive to the east for around 30 minutes from Tanjung Rhu Beach and you will arrive at Kuah Town which is located at south-eastern end of Langkawi Island. There are many hotels, various local restaurants and one of the biggest malls of "Langkawi Parade".

Langkawi Parade has a big supermarket at the basement. It may be the only one place you can buy fruits at Langkawi at the month of March. March and April are not the season of fruits at Langkawi, a taxi driver said like that. Therefore, if you want to get some fruits in March or in April, you have to go Langkawi Parade mall. It is located at the entrance of Kuah Town. Langkawi Parade is "潮 順 發" in Chinese and "Teow Soon Huat" in English. Address is "A14~15, Pokok Asam, Juah 07000 Pulau Langkawi, Malaysia" and Tel : 604 – 966-5017/5018.

City Bayview Hotel, Langkawi Baron Hotel and My Hotel which is introduced here, are located near each other. Attractions such as Jetty Point, Eagle Square and Legend Park, are near to Kuah Town.

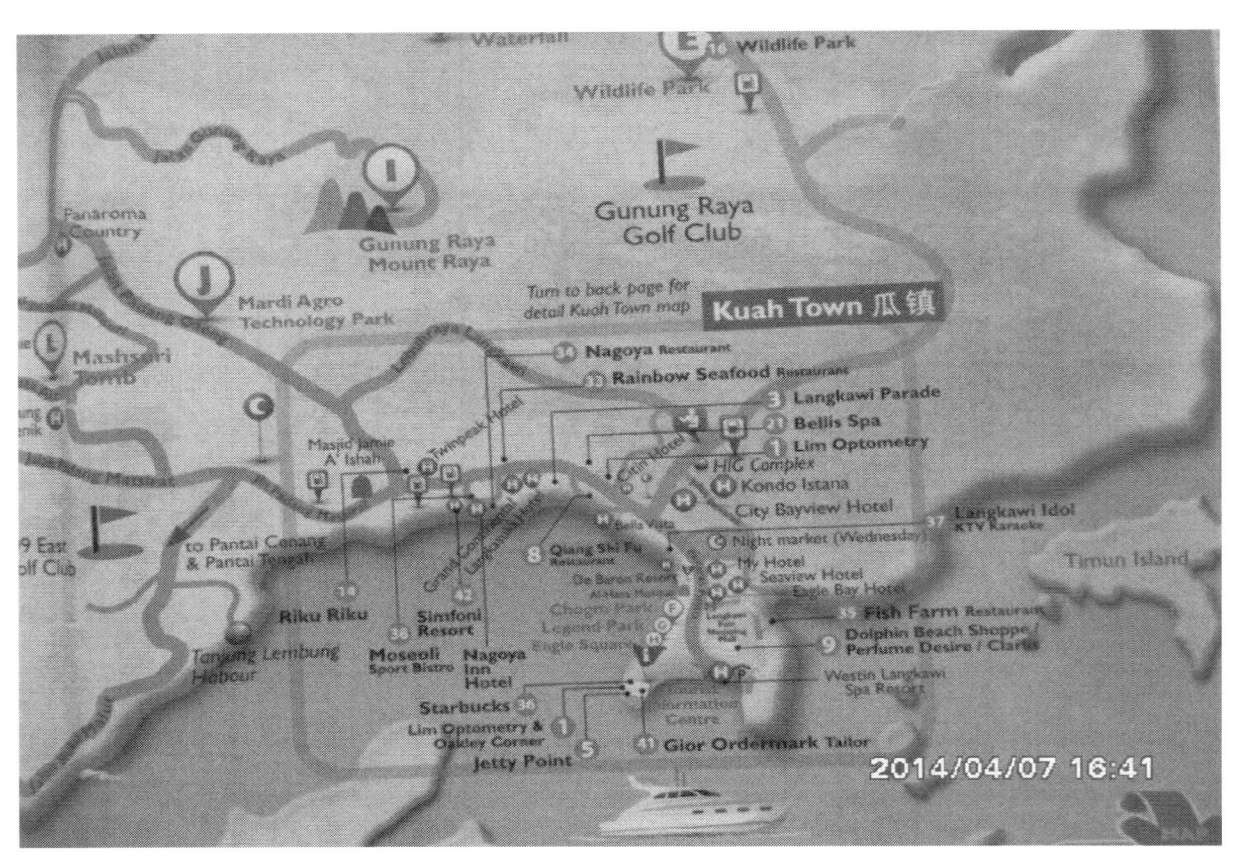

Kuah Town in the orange box. Hotels are centered on the right of the box. Jetty Point, Eagle Square, Legend Park and Chogm Park are concentrated at the bottom of the box.

Kuah Town looked down from the 3rd floor of My Hotel. The white building in front, is Bayview Hotel.

A road on the left seen from My Hotel, is running on a bridge towards Langkawi Parade mall.

The road you've seen from My Hotel. Go straight this road and you will meet Langkawi Parade, Pantai Cenang, airport and finally Oriental Village, too. If you come through this road and turn to the right as the arrow painted white on the road, you will meet My Hotel.

If you walk straight this road for around 20 minutes, you will find Langkawi Parade mall on you left. A KFC is located at the opposite side of the mall. If you follow the arrow painted white on the road, you will see Jetty Point and Eagle Square.

If you walk for around 20 minutes along the road, you will see the white building, Langkawi Parade, standing on the left. The only supermarket selling fruits in March at Langkawi, is situated at the basement of the mall. A KFC is near the mall.

Langkawi Parade.

Wrapping paper of Langkawi Parade. The mall is called "Teow Soon Suat" in Chinese.

KFC.

Inside of KFC.

The road looked back from KFC to the direction of Jetty Point.

The road to Langkawi Parade mall. Turn to the right with the house bearing a post of the king and the queen of Malaysia on your left and you will meet Bayview Hotel shortly.

You will see this scene when you turn to the right at the house.

Public telephone booth. They write "helo" instead of "hello". They also write "restoran" instead of "restaurant".

A bridge at the end of the road crowded with restaurants and shops. Baron Hotel is on the left and My Hotel is seen on the right.

My Hotel.

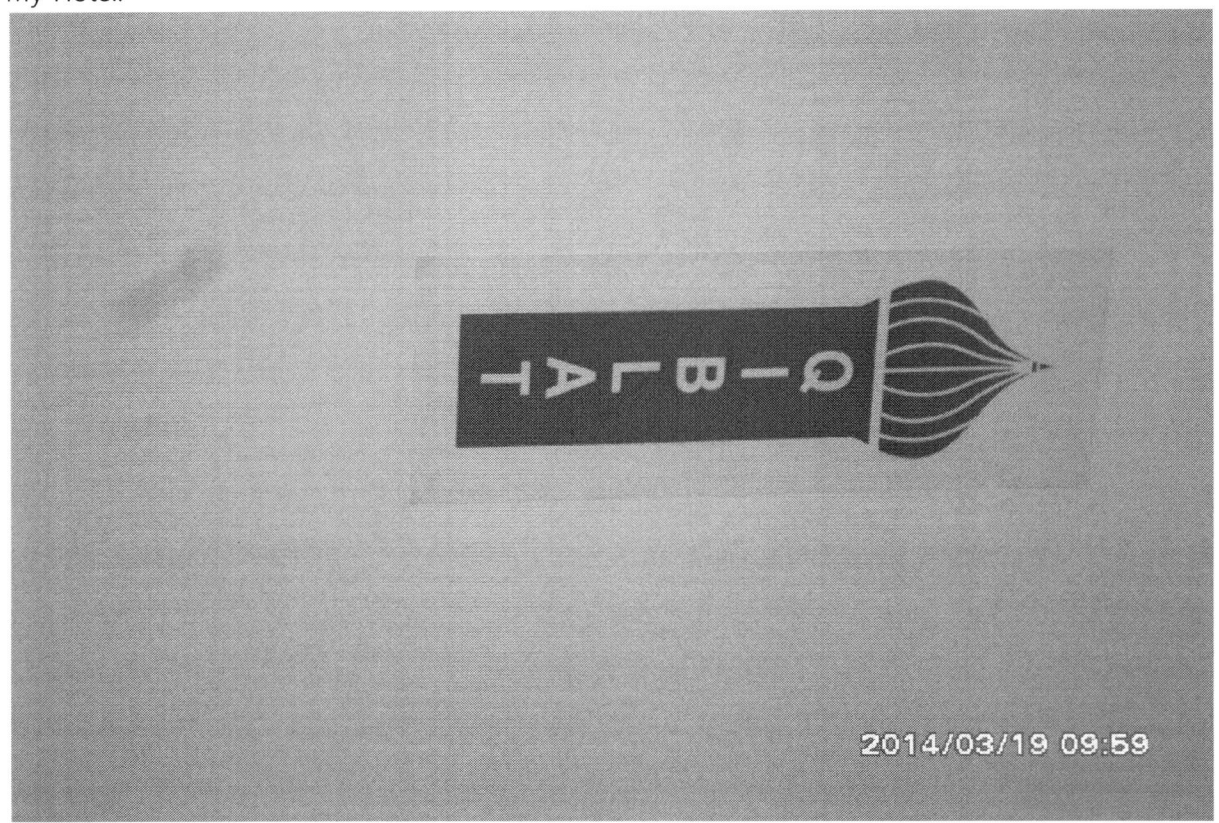

Sign for the Muslim prayers posted on the ceiling of hotel room. Direction to Mecca is one of the most important things for the prayers to bow.

A rent car parked at My Hotel. Baron Hotel is standing near My Hotel.

You are looking back the road crowded with restaurants and shops. The pink house on the left of the road, is a Chinese restaurant and the white building standing in front, is Bayview Hotel.

A Chinese restaurant at the pink house. Cheap and delicious.

Menu written in both Chinese and English.

A duty free shop at the opposite side of the Chinese restaurant. They sell various chocolate, tobacco and liquor.

All shops at Langkawi are duty free. However, you cannot easily find items except 3 kinds of goods at the stores. Chocolate, tobacco and liquor.

## (5) Eagle Square and Jetty Point

Jetty Point, a ferry terminal running to Penang and even to Thai islands, is located near Kuah Town. Eagle Square – eagle is the symbol of Langkawi – is connected with Jetty Point. After having lunch at food courts at Jetty Point, take a look at Eagle Square through a bridge from Jetty Point.

Many ticket agent offices are open at Jetty Point. Some of them sell tickets for the interstate buses going to Kuala Lumpur, Johor Bahru and Singapore as well.

Eagle Square connected with Jetty Point, has a giant statue of eagle looking just to fly to the sky at the bay front of the sea. There are a vast court, rest areas, viewpoints, a pond and beautiful houses at Eagle Square.

Ticket Agent Offices at Jetty Point.

You can park your car by the road in case of no empty at the parking lot of Jetty Point.

Sign board on a ferry ticket booth. 3 times a day running between Satun, Thailand and Langkawi, Malaysia.

Ticket office selling express bus tickets towards Kuala Lumpur, Ipoh, Melaka, Johor Bahru and Singapore as well.

Food Court. They serve various kinds of food from various countries.

A bridge at the food court linked to Eagle Square.

On the bridge to Eagle Square.

Eagle statue under the blue sky.

Tourists are going to the bay front to take a photo of the statue.

Ready to take off.

Eagle is the symbol of Langkawi.

Travelers are photographing at bay front.

The Pythagoras' triangle. No word except "fantastic".

You are looking back to Jetty Point from Eagle statue.

A yard by the pond.

You can take a rest on the chair at the white building.

Inside of the white building.

Parking lot filled with countless cars at Jetty Point.

Food court at Jetty Point.

Outside of the food court. The bridge is seen between red parasols.

A lucky sparrow on a dish.

## (6) Legend Park & Chogm Park

Legend Park and Chogm Park are situated near Jetty Point. The two parks are connected each other. In 5 minutes from Jetty Point by a car, you will get the parks. They are green heavens. Walking and jogging would really match with the roads well organized in the parks.

Entry to Legend Park.

Map of Langkawi Island engraved on the rocks at the entrance.

To the park.

People are strolling in the park early in the morning.

A well organized promenade by a pond.

Perfect to take a walk and jogging.

Beautiful flowers are thriving on the right side of the promenade. This is the end of my introduction for the wonderful island of "Langkawi".

Printed in Germany
by Amazon Distribution
GmbH, Leipzig